A Guide To Style

Jim McMillan

1-9-06

A Guide To Style

A MANUAL FOR BUSINESS AND PROFESSIONAL WOMEN

IRIS McMILLAN

LOGANFIELD, INC.

ISBN: 0-9679588-0-6
Library of Congress Catalog Number: 00-190314

Although the author and publisher have made every effort to ensure the accuracy and completeness of information contained in this book, we assume no responsibility for errors, inaccuracies, omissions or any inconsistency herein. Any slights of people, products or organizations are unintentional.

Book Cover Design: Iris McMillan
Figure on Cover: Carol Taggart
Illustrations: Rifka Barth
Typesetting and Formatting: Susy Willis

Published by
Loganfield, Inc.
P. O. Box 3984
Tallahassee, FL 32315-3984
Printed in the United States of America

Beauty in style and grace depend on simplicity.

—Plato

Contents

Introduction to Style...1

Chapter 1

Style in Three Frames...5

Chapter 2

The Larger Frame..9
    Attitude..11
    Voice..12

Chapter 3

Framing Your Face..13
    Hairstyle...16
    Earrings..18
    Color Closest to Face..............................19

Chapter 4

The Face in the Frame..21
    Skin Care..22
    Face Care..24
    Makeup...25
        Makeup Consultation........................25
        Purchasing Cosmetics........................28
        Makeup Application...........................28

Foundation, Concealer, and Powder 29
Lips...29
Eyebrows...30
Eyelashes...31
Eyeshadow...31
Eyeliner..31
Blusher 31

Chapter 5
Fragrances...33

Chapter 6
Nails...37

Chapter 7
Framing Your Body..41
Framing Front and Back...................................44
Framing Side...44
Framing with Clothing Design and Color........................46
Dealing with Figure Flaws.................................47
Weight Problems..47

Chapter 8
Wardrobe..49
Wardrobe Inventory...52
Coordination of Wardrobe Colors...............................53
Basic Wardrobe Color Groups.........................53
Your Wardrobe Colors 54
Caucasian Women.......................................54
Warm Colors...54

Cool Colors..55
Women of Color..55
Warm Colors...55
Cool Colors..55
Expanded List of Colors..............................55
Jewel Tones..57
Neutral Colors...57
Coordinated Ensembles...............................57
Black Outfits...57
Brown Outfits...59
Navy Outfits..61
Prints, Patterns, and Plaids.........................64
Wardrobe Lists..65
Barebones Wardrobe.................................65
Wardrobe Building List..............................66
Evening Wardrobe...................................67
Travel Wardrobe.....................................71
Wardrobe Pieces......................................72
Suits...72
Dresses..75
Jackets...78
Pants...82
Skirts...85
Blouses, Sweaters, and Shirts......................87
Blouses..87
Sweaters...88
Shirts..90
Coats...91

Chapter 9

Accessories...93
Handbags...96
Shoes..99
Pantyhose...100

Belts..101
Gloves...102
Scarves..102
Jewelry...104
Watches...107
Eyewear...107

Chapter 10

Shopping...109

Chapter 11

Becoming a Woman of Style....................................115

Don'ts...119

Index..125

Notes..131

Orders..133

Introduction

to

Style

Introduction

To

Style

The style's the woman, anyhow.

—Oliver Wendell Holmes

Style, as the term is used in this book, means the distinctively attractive manner in which you present yourself to the world; the overall image of captivating individuality you project to others. It can be almost magical in its effect.

A classy style stands out! You know it when you see it. Virtually any woman can develop it if she is receptive to instruction and dedicated to the effort, and this effort will save a lot of expensive trial and error.

The woman with an attractive and engaging personal style has a magnetic presence, perhaps even charisma. She compensates for any lack of natural beauty with her self-confident, upbeat attitude and in the way she is dressed and groomed. She obviously cares for herself as well as others and brightens her surroundings for all to enjoy. The message is clear. She demonstrates her respect for those around her and seeks to gain their attention and respect by the way she dresses and the manner in which she presents herself. Her style is never careless, not even on casual, dress-down Fridays.

Style cannot be guaranteed by the amount of money spent nor the number of outfits in your closet. It is a matter of studied, cultivated taste. Style includes the right choices in clothes, colors, accessories, makeup, and hairstyle, as well as posture, carriage, voice, and attitude. It is a combination of fundamentals with touches of current fashion trends. All of these are discussed in this book.

The following ideas and suggestions concerning the development of your personal style are basic and conservative and do not purport to cover everything. They are presented to provide you with a foundation upon which you may develop your own special style. Study and expand upon them as your confidence grows.

Now, read on to develop the style that is right for *you*, the working woman of whatever age or occupational level, to whom this book is dedicated.

Chapter 1

Style

in

Three Frames

Style

in

Three Frames

Begin the development of your own personal style by visualizing yourself in three frames: a frame for your face, a frame for your body, and a larger frame of the manner in which you present yourself to the world.

The fundamental purpose of the first two frames is to create pleasing outlines to balance the proportions of your face and your body. Your face is framed by your hairstyle, earrings, and the necklace or color worn closest to your face. Your body is framed by the undergarments, clothing designs, colors, and accessories you wear.

The third and largest imaginary frame contains your framed face complete with natural-looking makeup, your framed body attractively attired to further balance your proportions and, for the finishing touch, the engaging aura of the manner in which you present these assets to the world.

Chapter 2

The Larger Frame

The

Larger

Frame

Some women, the few, have charm for all . . . .

—James Matthew Barrie

The larger frame brings everything together and adds the charm, including a pleasant voice and self-confident attitude.

Attitude

A positive and self-confident attitude is essential to the development and maintenance of an attractive personal style. One of the most effective ways to project such an attitude is to be well-groomed and well-dressed. Looking good makes you feel better and more confident about yourself and that feeling is transmitted naturally to those with whom you come in contact.

Another effective way to project an attitude of self confidence is by your posture and the way in which you carry yourself. Consider the attitude your posture and carriage portray to others and try to correct any hints of apathy or negativism. Show your spirit! Stand tall, chin up, eyes bright and expectant. Roll your shoulders back, pull your tummy in, your derriere under, and walk with a smooth, gliding gait. And smile! This sends a message of self confidence like nothing else. (As the saying goes, no woman is completely dressed until she is wearing a smile.)

What you wear under your clothes plays a vital role in your posture and largely determines how well you wear your clothes. Properly fitted undergarments make a significant difference in firming the hips and tummy, slimming the thighs and lifting the bust, all of which improve your posture as well as your overall look. Most major department stores and lingerie shops can fit you properly with the right undergarments.

Voice

It is important to recognize the significant impact your voice can have on others. A shrill, nasal, loud, or otherwise unpleasant voice can greatly detract from your personal style. Consequently, you should speak distinctly and correctly in the softer, perhaps lower, registers. A softer voice usually gains more attention and respect than a loud one. Laughter should never be boisterous, too frequent, or extended in duration. And avoid the use of profanity; it is never becoming and often reveals a lack of self-confidence.

Chapter 3

Framing Your Face

Framing Your Face

When others first meet you, your face is naturally the center of their attention. It is where they first look to evaluate who you are and what they perhaps should think of you. Consequently, you should make every effort to enhance the appearance of your face. You get only one chance to make a first impression and first impressions are often lasting impressions.

Once a good impression is made, the objective in the workplace is to direct attention to your face rather than your figure. To do this, you must first frame your face properly. As previously noted, this is accomplished by your selection of hairstyle, earrings, and the necklace or color worn closest to your face.

Hairstyle

To properly frame your face, your hairstyle must be balanced and proportionate to the shape and size of your face and body.

Ideally, our foreheads should not be too high, nor our faces too long, round, or square. But the perfectly proportioned face is rare, and most of us have to rely on hairstyle, among other things, to bring our features into better balance.

The variety of facial shapes and constantly changing fashion in hairstyles make it impossible to prescribe *one* hairstyle for anyone, but balance should be kept foremost in mind when choosing a hairstyle. Some common-sense examples include the following: bangs of some sort for high foreheads; fuller on the sides and less full on top for long faces; fuller on top and less full on the sides for round or square faces. Perfect balance, however, is not necessarily the goal. Indeed, the overall shape of your hairstyle should tend more toward the triangular than the shape of a football helmet. Look for pictures of fashionable hairstyles you think might work for you and save them to show your hairstylist.

Medium Bob

Your decision on hair length should be easy. Long hair is for the young. The most attractive and manageable length is a fashionable, medium bob that falls between the ears and shoulders. Within that range, the hair should generally be longer and fuller for the tall, slim, or young; shorter and less full for the petite, heavy, or older woman. But do not forget the rule that the larger the woman, the larger the hair. However, this never means "Big Hair"!

Your haircut is fundamental to the way your hair will ultimately look. Indeed, your haircut *is* your hairstyle. Without a good haircut you can never have a good hairstyle. With a good haircut your hairstyle should fall into place even when allowed to air-dry. Consequently, you should have an expert hairstylist cut your hair.

Expert hairstylists are often hard to find. Get recommendations from those you see with outstanding hairstyles. Even with such recommendations, you may experience some trial and error before finding the hairstylist who consistently cuts and styles your hair for the look and ease of care you want.

Discuss with your hairstylist how your hair can be attractively styled to frame your face. If you have pictures of fashionable hairstyles you think will work for you, show them to him or her. Once you and your hairstylist have decided on a hairstyle and you are happy with the results, ask the stylist for pointers on how to do your hair at home. Then you may return to the stylist only when you need a haircut.

Keep your hair soft and shiny by shampooing and conditioning once or twice a week. But do not use a conditioner if your hair is fine or thin; it reduces the body.

Earrings

Earrings must be proportionate to the shape of your face, neck-length and body size. A petite woman should not wear heavy earrings, nor should a large woman wear tiny earrings. A good rule is to wear the largest earrings your proportions and other jewelry will accommodate in good balance. Do not be timid!

Hoop

Another good rule is to contrast the shape of your earrings with the shape of your face. For example, squarish for round faces, and roundish for square faces. Wide hoops do well with both.

Drop

Earring length should be proportionate to neck length: buttons for shorter necks, hoops and drops for longer necks. The longer the neck, the longer the earrings.

Wide hoops, short drops, and buttons in plain gold or silver are good earrings for the working woman. Save the glitter and sparkle for evening.

Button

Sparkling earrings may be drops, hoops, buttons, or studs in crystal, rhinestones, diamonds, or any gemstone, synthetic or real. Pearl earrings also are appropriate for evening.

Color Closest To Face

To complete the framing of your face, the color worn closest to your face may be the color of your blouse, sweater, shirt, or jacket (if worn with a camisole). Accent colors particularly will call attention to your face, as will a collar necklace or any other short bold necklace in gold or silver.

Your final decision on color should be made by holding the color next to your face, perhaps under your chin, in natural light. (Beware of yellow next to your face unless you have a drop-dead tan, natural or acquired.)

Chapter 4

The Face
in the
Frame

The Face
in the
Frame

Once you have created the right frame for your face, you must take the necessary steps to make sure it surrounds a face that has a natural look and is skillfully made-up to balance and enhance your facial features.

Skin Care

Your goal in skin care is to have clean, moist, smooth skin. The variety of products to help you achieve this is almost infinite. But the most important ingredient in all these products is the moisturizing element, the purpose of which is to avoid dry skin and thereby prevent wrinkles.

Exposure to the sun is the major cause of dry skin and wrinkling, which lead to the premature appearance of aging. It is therefore important to guard against the harmful rays.

Popular sun screens include *Oil of Olay's Daily Moisturizer with Z Cote* and *Neutrogena Moisturizer with SPF 15*. But even with a good sun screen, you should never expose your skin to the sun for extended periods of time. The longer you are in the sun, the less effective the sun screen.

Among the cremes for reducing (not removing) wrinkles are *Nivea's Q 10 Wrinkle Control Face Cream, St. Ives Wrinkle Control Face Cream, L'Oréal's Plenitude Revitalift Anti-Wrinkle + Firming Cream,* and *Renova* (by prescription). Those with sensitive skin may want to try *Pond's Age Defying Complex* or *L'Oréal's Turning Point.* Alternatively, you may have an acid-peel done by a plastic surgeon or plastic surgeon's nurse practitioner. You may choose the one-step medical acid-peel or the milder four-step medical procedure.

Remember, style is about looking good, whatever your age!

Face Care

To keep your face looking good at any age, you should regularly follow a three-step routine of cleansing, exfoliating and moisturizing, particularly before applying makeup.

> (1) Wash your face with a non-abrasive soap like *Clinique's Face Bar* or a cleanser such as *Cetaphil's Gentle Skin Cleanser.* Use your hands to lather, rinse thoroughly, and then pat dry.

> (2) To exfoliate (remove dead skin), apply an astringent, clarifying lotion or toner such as *Nivea's Visage, Alpha Hydrox Toner/Astrin-*

gent, or *Clinique's Clarifying Lotion*, suitable for your skin type (dry, normal, or oily).

(3) Moisturize your face with a rich moisturizing lotion or creme such as those made by *Alpha Hydrox, Oil of Olay, L'Oréal, Revlon, Clinique* or *Lancome*.

For best results, repeat this process morning and night.

Makeup

Your makeup colors include the colors of your foundation, powder, blusher, eyeshadow, eyeliner, eyebrow pencil, lipliner, lipstick, and nail polish. Determining your best makeup colors and appropriate application procedures requires a complete assessment of your face, including the colors of your hair, eyes, and skin, and the shape of your face. This assessment will dictate not only the best colors for your makeup and how it should be applied, but also the colors of the clothes you should wear.

There are, of course, numerous variations in the colors of hair, eyes, and skin, but the basic colors are:

Hair: Blonde, Red, Brown, Black, Gray

Eyes: Blue, Green, Hazel, Brown

Skin: Fair, Medium Fair, Olive, Medium Olive, Dark Olive, Black

Makeup Consultation

In most major department stores, each cosmetics counter will offer, by appointment, a free color consultation and make-over. Based on the colors of your hair, eyes, and skin, some of the consultants will use a computer to determine your best range of colors, while others will make the determination by sight. Neither method is necessarily superior to the other. It all depends upon the expertise of the consultant, which varies from counter to counter and store to store. Whatever the method used, your consultant will identify your hair, eye, and skin colors, and your all-important skin tone.

Among Caucasian women, there are generally two basic skin tones: yellow-orange and blue-red. Blondes and redheads with blue, green, or hazel eyes and fair to medium-fair skin usually have a yellow-orange skin tone and should wear both makeup and clothing in *warm* colors. Those with brown or black hair, and brown, blue, green, or hazel eyes with olive skin usually have a blue-red skin tone and should wear both makeup and clothing in *cool* colors.

Women of color similarly have two basic skin tones: yellow and red. Those with a yellow skin tone should wear both makeup and clothing in *warm* colors, and those with a red skin tone should wear makeup and clothing in *cool* colors.

Some women have skin tones that are adaptable to wearing either warm or cool colors. For them, it is best to determine first their most obvious category and later experiment with colors in the other category. Whatever their choice, both makeup and clothes should always be in either warm or cool colors, not a mix of both. For instance, coral makeup (particularly lipstick and blusher) should never be worn with pink clothes, and vice versa.

The range of warm and cool colors for clothing include not only the warm and cool makeup color ranges but much more. Warm colors in clothing, for example, include yellow-greens, while cool colors for clothing include blue-greens.

Upon completion of your make-over, the consultant should furnish you with a chart or booklet listing your best colors for foundation, concealer, powder, blusher, eyeshadow, eyeliner, lipliner, and lipstick. She also should tell you whether your colors are warm or cool, identify the shape of your face, and instruct you in the procedures for applying your makeup.

If you have any lingering doubts after your first consultation, do not hesitate to seek the opinions of consultants at other cosmetic counters or even an independent makeup specialist who will, of course, charge you a fee.

Whatever you do, obtain sufficient consultation to be confident in the results before buying makeup or a new wardrobe. Remember, your wardrobe and makeup colors should be in the same color range, and one of your primary purposes in going to a makeup consultant is to determine the range of your best makeup colors and whether that color range is *warm* or *cool*.

Some discretion will be left to you to decide whether you prefer the lighter or darker shades in your particular makeup color range. A good rule for choosing the lightness or darkness of the shades is to make your selections consistent with the lightness or darkness of your hair, eyes, and skin.

Using a capable makeup consultant is unquestionably the best way to select your best makeup color range and to learn the correct use and application of cleansers, astringents, moisturizers, and makeup. Makeup fashions change, so return for an update every year or so.

Purchasing Cosmetics

Cosmetics such as concealer, foundation, powder, eye makeup, blusher, lipstick, liners, and skin care products are readily available at both department and drug stores. The price of cosmetics covers a wide range and you do not necessarily have to buy expensive brands to get good ones. Price has little to do, for example, with how lipsticks perform. Look for those cosmetics that fit your budget and select the ones you like. Some excellent and perhaps pricier brands are *Clinique, Lancome, Estée Lauder, Elizabeth Arden, and Prescriptives.* Less expensive brands often found in drug stores include *Ultima II, Revlon, Maybelline, L'Oréal, Max Factor, Almay,* and *Cover Girl.* All of these are of good quality and provide quite satisfactory results. Many of these brands also offer cosmetic brushes at reasonable prices.

Some good, lower-priced cleansers are *Cetaphil Skin Cleanser, Neutrogena Skin Cleanser,* and *Oil of Olay Foaming Face Wash.* Lower priced astringents/toners include *Nivea Visage, Alpha Hydrox Toner/Astringent,* and *Revlon Moon Drops.* Lower priced moisturizers include those by *Almay, Clarins, Oil of Olay, Revlon,* and *Cetaphil.*

Makeup Application

The shape of your face will determine the manner in which you apply your makeup. There are perhaps a dozen variously described facial shapes, but the five basic shapes are round, oval, long, square, and heart-shaped. Your makeup consultant will identify your facial shape and instruct you in the appropriate makeup application procedures. Always ask for a customized chart with a list of your makeup colors.

Your dressing table equipment should include a magnifying or electric makeup mirror, a brush collection (including powder, blusher, lip, eyeshadow, eyebrow, eyelash, and lip brushes), and a sponge for applying your foundation. With guidance from your makeup consultant and a little practice, you should be able to apply your makeup in little more than ten minutes. This short time will be spent to great advantage. Develop the habit of doing it every morning. In addition to enhancing your personal style, it will make you feel better as you start each new day!

Foundation, Concealer, and Powder

Your concealer is applied first, but the most important item in your makeup is the *foundation!* It should match your skin as perfectly as possible. You must let it dry *completely* before applying powder and other makeup. Always use a translucent powder, if any at all.

Lips

Lips may be perfect, too full, too thin, or just too something. In any case, a lip pencil sharpened to a fine point is the best tool for creating a beautiful outline and correcting any flaws. Choose the colors of your lip pencil and your lipstick together. The lipstick should be in a slightly lighter shade than the pencil.

Apply light foundation and powder to your lips and use the lip pencil to create the lipline you want. For full lips, the line should be just inside the natural lipline. For thin lips, the line should be just outside the natural lipline.

For uneven lips, the line should be outside the natural line where uneven and the uneven area filled in with lip pencil.

Older women may want to apply moisturizer and concealer around the mouth, foundation over the concealer, and a light dusting of powder before applying liner and lipstick. Older women also should use the lighter shades of lipstick and lipliner.

After applying lipliner, fill in the lips with lipstick in a slightly lighter shade, directly from the tube or with a lip brush.

Avoid using dark eye makeup when using a dark lip color. Use one or the other to call attention to your best feature, but never both. If, however, both features are outstanding, just alternate from time to time, you lucky girl!

Full lips, together with large eyes and gracefully arched eyebrows, are keys to feminine attractiveness.

Eyebrows

Your eyebrows are vital to your overall appearance and can detract strongly from your other features if not properly sized and shaped. It is astonishing how dark, heavy eyebrows can instantly become the focal point of the face.

Your eyebrows should always have a balanced, finished look. Avoid the painted look by using a light taupe or light brown, sharp-pointed eyebrow pencil to shape and fill in your eyebrows. Your makeup consultant is the best source of assistance in properly sizing and arching your eyebrows.

Eyelashes

Use an eyelash curler and mascara to make your lashes look longer and thicker, or use one of the newer mascaras that curl your lashes while it thickens them. *Maybelline Great Lash* and *Prescriptives Lashes Gentle* are good mascara choices.

Eyeshadow

The best eyeshadow colors are brown, taupe, or gray. They go with any eye color. Apply concealer or foundation around the eye area (including under the eyes), color the entire lid with light eyeshadow, and contour the crease with medium to dark eyeshadow. Avoid blue, purple, and green eyeshadow.

Eyeliner

Eyeliner defines the eyes but should never be dark. A soft natural brown or gray is best. It may be applied to both upper and lower lids, but it often detracts when on the lower lid if not sparingly and expertly applied.

Eye makeup, properly applied, can enhance the size and appearance of your eyes, but overuse of eye makeup is the surest way to get the "painted lady" look. So when in doubt, always understate your eye makeup.

Blusher

Blusher should be the last makeup you apply because the appropriate intensity of your blusher will depend upon the colors you wear near your face. If those colors are pale, your blusher should be more intense. If those colors are bright, you should apply less blusher, or none at all.

Chapter 5

Fragrances

Fragrances

Less is more. Delicacy is the objective in using fragrances. The subtlety is not only more appealing; it also is more considerate of those around you, particularly in the workplace and for those who have allergies.

Perfumes are preferable to colognes, which cost less but fade fast. Choose a light and airy, perhaps floral, perfume for summer, and a bit heavier scent for winter.

You do not have to restrict yourself to famous brands to get an exquisite perfume. The choices are virtually limitless and can be readily sampled at perfume counters, so carefully choose a fetching, subtle, and distinctive one. Discount stores such as *T J Maxx* and *Ross* often have good selections at reasonable prices.

Do not mix fragrances. Avoid scented cosmetics when using perfume. Apply perfume lightly to your inner arms above the wrist and to the back of your neck, not to your clothing.

Chapter 6

Nails

Nails

Your hands are as noticeable as your face and require equal attention. Neglecting the appearance of your hands can be damaging to a finished look.

Regular manicures are essential, whether done by you or a professional. Your nail polish color may be chosen from your makeup color range, although platinum polish and French manicures are always elegant, whatever your makeup colors.

Acrylic nails are preferred by many, and for good reason. They look marvelous (if not too long), and the initial set is relatively inexpensive. Fill-ins, however, are required every two to three weeks. The polish never chips and your hands always look great, provided you have otherwise taken care of them.

Moisturize your hands twice a day with a good moisturizer such as *Neutrogena Body Emulsion.* You also, on occasion, might rub your hands with almond oil in the evening and wear cotton gloves overnight. This softens and smooths the hands marvelously.

Give yourself a pedicure once a month. All it takes is a tube or jar of nail treatment creme, nail clippers, polish, and a few minutes. Before bedtime, trim your toenails and rub them with the nail treatment cream. Next morning apply platinum polish or the same color as your fingernails and you are ready to go!

Chapter 7

Framing Your Body

Framing Your Body

Our bodies come in an almost infinite variety of shapes, sizes, and proportions. When our proportions are not as perfect as we would like, we can use undergarments, shoulder pads, clothing design, prints and patterns, colors, and accessories to detract from our less attractive features, highlight our best features, and create an overall balanced look.

Looking our best often requires the balancing of one part of the body against another. In our society that usually means making the body appear as slim and uniform as possible. To accomplish this, the body must be framed from the side as well as the front and back.

Framing the Front and Back

The front and back of the body are framed primarily by balancing the width of the shoulders with the hips. Most feminine shoulders are not as wide as the hips, so shoulder pads, dropped-shoulder sleeves, and epaulettes are some corrective clothing features.

Plain, ordinary shoulder pads can work miracles in framing the body. The appropriate size of shoulder pads depends upon the slope of the shoulders and the extension needed to balance the hips. For jackets, the pads should be squared-off to extend and smooth the area from the neck to the tip of the extended shoulder. For garments of softer fabric, a rounded shoulder pad works best.

Jackets, of course, will come with shoulder pads, but you will often need to buy rounded shoulder pads for sweaters and blouses. Shop for these at fabric stores. Make sure the pads are the appropriate size and shape for your body-framing purposes.

Framing the Side

Framing the body from the side often requires correcting for a protruding tummy and derriere. Some undergarments that may be helpful in balancing this profile are control-top pantyhose, support pantyhose, uplift bra, girdle, waist nipper, thigh slimmer, the all-in-one waist nipper/girdle/thigh slimmer, the body slip, or the all-in-one body shaper.

44

Framing the Body with Shoulder Pads

Framing with Clothing Design and Color

Framing the body is not confined to the use of undergarments. There are other solutions that distract the eye rather than restrict the body. These may be condensed into such basic principles as the following:

- Vertical lines in clothing design or patterned fabrics are slimming.

- Horizontal lines in clothing design or patterned fabrics enlarge and broaden the areas where they occur.

- Dark colors tend to minimize the size of the areas they cover.

- Light colors tend to maximize the size of the areas they cover.

- Light or bright colored areas draw attention away from dark colored areas.

- Light colors above the waist draw attention away from dark colors below the waist.

- Prints and patterns draw attention away from solid colored areas.

- Using the same color head-to-toe is slimming.

- Tone-on-tone separates are slimming.

- Long necklaces and long hoop earrings are slimming.

- Tight-fitting clothes exaggerate the features they cover.

- Soft fabrics cover and soften figure flaws better than hard-finish fabrics.

- Heavy fabrics, patch pockets, loose pleats, and ruffles add bulk.

Dealing With Figure Flaws

Chances are, your figure flaws are not as serious or as hopeless as you might imagine. It is important not to exaggerate them in your own mind and let them become an obsession. This is a common, self-defeating trap. If you dwell too much on your figure flaws, you likely will make the mistake of neglecting your best features. Take a more positive approach.

Study the body framing methods already discussed, determine those clothing designs, colors, patterns, and undergarments that most effectively minimize your figure flaws, and use them on a regular and continuing basis. You then can stop agonizing over how to conceal or camouflage your figure flaws and concentrate your creative efforts on enhancing your best features. The enhancement of such features as your face and hair will further minimize figure flaws by diverting attention from them to your better features.

Weight Problems

Excessive weight, frankly, is usually the result of excessive eating. To lose weight, you usually must eat less. This is easier said than done because it requires more than the sporadic exercise of will power. There must be a fundamental change in attitude toward food. (Consult your physician, however, before undertaking the loss of substantial weight.)

The desire for something else must be greater than the desire for food. So if you are overweight, why not make that "something else" your determination to further develop your own classy style! Such motivation, if strong enough, could lessen the ordeal of losing weight. A simple but effective diet plan is to consume at each meal only the quantity of food that can be placed within the inner ring of your dinner plate.

The excessive consumption of food is often a short-term pleasure that causes the long-term "pain" of excess weight. An attractive figure, on the other hand, enhances an attractive personal style that provides long-term plea-sures far beyond any fleeting culinary delights.

Until the excess weight is lost, however, things can be done to minimize the appearance of being overweight. The most obvious tactic is to wear loose-fitting clothes of soft fabric. Wear jackets, vests, tunics, and other tops that fall easily over the lower torso and hips. Coat dresses em-phasize the vertical (slimming) line. Long hoop earrings and long necklaces are helpful in further emphasizing the vertical line. Light-weight, non-clinging fabrics reduce bulk.

Clothes in dark solid colors with shoes and hose of the same color also are slimming. Use scarves and jewelry to add color and draw attention to your face.

Chapter 8

Wardrobe

Wardrobe

A modest woman, dressed out in all her finery, is the most tremendous object of the whole creation.

—Oliver Goldsmith

Keep you wardrobe simple. A good wardrobe is one with clothes you enjoy that can be worn in different combinations. Getting the most from your wardrobe means learning to tastefully mix a few pieces for many occasions. The ability to mix and match everything in your closet is the definition of a good wardrobe.

Building a wardrobe is a continuing process. You should first acquire the basic pieces (suits, dresses, jackets, skirts, and pants). Then, as your budget permits, expand your wardrobe by collecting assorted blouses, sweaters, shirts and accessories.

Building a wardrobe for a polished, professional look should be one of your prime goals as a working woman. In addition to applying the knowledge gained from books such as this, you should observe the dress and manner of the women who hold senior positions in your workplace. This will provide you with some idea of the style you need to develop to succeed in that particular environment. A good rule is to dress to the level just above you.

Whether self-employed or an employee, the woman who is visible to the public necessarily becomes a part of the image her company projects to its customers. A refined image naturally attracts, while a careless or slovenly appearance repels. Consequently, any company that wants to remain viable must provide greater opportunities and rewards to those who enhance, rather than detract from, the company's image. The successful woman understands this, determines what the company needs from her, and adapts accordingly. Both appearance and productivity are often fundamental to advancement.

The woman in the workplace who dresses to direct attention to her face and demonstrates good taste in her clothes and manner usually will be held in higher esteem by her co-workers, employer, and the company's customers or clients.

Wardrobe Inventory

Before you do any serious shopping, take an inventory of your existing wardrobe. First, discard those pieces that cannot be updated or no longer fit, and those you no longer like. Then, make a written inventory of what is left and formulate your basic wardrobe plan. (Suggested wardrobe lists begin at page 65.)

This inventory will show you where your wardrobe is deficient and enable you to make a list of what you need to complete your basic wardrobe plan. Everything you purchase thereafter should be consistent with that plan and mix well with the retained pieces in your existing wardrobe.

Coordination of Wardrobe Colors

Color produces remarkable effects when used properly. The right choices of color can, among other things, help frame your face and balance your body proportions, as well as provide variety and versatility to expand your wardrobe. The proper use and coordination of colors, however, must be based on an adequate knowledge of makeup colors and basic wardrobe color groups.

Basic Wardrobe Color Groups

Your basic wardrobe colors should be chosen from one of three color groups:

Black Group

Black, White, Camel, Cream, Beige, Tan, Taupe, Silver, Gray

Brown Group

Brown, Pale Yellow, Cream, Wheat, Beige, Camel, Tan, Gold

Navy Group

Navy, White, Camel, Cream, Beige, Tan, Taupe, Silver, Gray

All your basic wardrobe pieces — suits, jackets, dresses with jackets, skirts, and pants — should be in either *solid black, solid brown,* or *solid navy.* Once you have obtained your core wardrobe pieces in one of these solid colors, additional pieces in other colors from your basic wardrobe color group may be added to enhance your mix and match capabilities.

Black is the ultimate wardrobe color. It is elegant, slimming, and right for all occasions. But whatever the basic wardrobe color you choose, be sure the shades match when buying separates.

Your Wardrobe Colors

Once you have chosen your wardrobe color group and acquired your basic pieces in black, brown, or navy, the colors of your other clothing should be chosen from the neutral colors in your wardrobe color group and your warm or cool accent colors. If your makeup colors are in the *warm* color range, your other clothing should be in *warm* and neutral colors. If your makeup colors are in the *cool* color range, your other clothing should be in *cool* and neutral colors. (See pages 25-27 regarding makeup colors.)

Some basic wardrobe, neutral, and accent colors that will coordinate with warm or cool makeup colors are as follows:

Caucasian Women

Warm Colors (Yellow-Orange Skin Tone)

Basic Wardrobe and Neutral Colors: BROWN or BLACK with Ivory, Cream, White, Tan, Beige, Camel

Accent Colors: Coral, Tomato Red, Garnet, Brick, Gold, Olive

Cool Colors (Blue-Red Skin Tone)

Basic Wardrobe and Neutral Colors: NAVY or BLACK with White, Ivory, Cream, Beige, Taupe, Silver, Gray

Accent Colors: Cranberry, Ruby, Fuchsia, Plum, Sapphire

Women of Color

Warm Colors (Yellow Skin Tone)

Basic Wardrobe and Neutral Colors: BROWN or BLACK with White, Ivory, Cream, Beige, Tan, Camel

Accent Colors: Coral, Tomato Red, Salmon, Olive, Yellow, Gold, Terra Cotta, Brick

Cool Colors (Red Skin Tone)

Basic Wardrobe and Neutral Colors: NAVY or BLACK with White, Cream, Ivory, Beige, Camel, Taupe

Accent Colors: Cranberry, Blue-Reds, Plum, Burgundy, Royal Blue, Sapphire

With your clothes and makeup in the same color range, anything in your wardrobe will go with your makeup. This will enable you to apply your makeup before making the final selection of the clothes you will wear.

Expanded List of Colors

Basically, color-coordination requires an ability to identify warm and cool colors and which category you should wear. The following lists of warm and cool colors, although not exhaustive, may be used for quick reference when making color choices:

Warm Colors	Cool Colors
Coral	Hot Pink
Salmon	Rose
Pumpkin	Mauve
Peach	Rosewood
Tomato Red	Fuchsia
Garnet	Purple
Orange-Reds	Ruby
Rust	Cranberry
Terra Cotta	Burgundy
Brick	Blue-Reds
Amber	Plum
Apple Green	Maroon
Jade	Aqua
Olive	Emerald
Turquoise	Teal
Yellow	Sky Blue
Gold	Sapphire
Mustard	Pale Gray
Warm Brown	Blue Gray
Dark Brown	Navy

Jewel Tones

Jewel tones are variations of gemstone colors, although they are not always referred to in gemstone terms. Some warm jewel tones are garnet, gold (citrine), jade, and turquoise. Cool jewel tones include ruby, emerald, sapphire, and purple (amethyst).

Neutral Colors

Neutral colors such as white, oyster, ivory, cream, camel, tan, and taupe are both warm and cool. Other colors that may also qualify as warm or cool include teal, jade, emerald, and turquoise.

Coordinated Ensembles

Some color-coordinated outfits you may put together are listed below with additional mixing and matching suggestions. You may confidently wear any of these combinations (according to your skin tone) for work or a job interview.

Black Outfits

Black and Ivory
(neutral)

Black suit (pants or skirt), black shoes, Barely Black pantyhose, and black handbag with:

Ivory blouse (notched collar or jewel-neckline) or ivory sweater (crewneck or turtleneck)

Gold hoop earrings

Gold collar necklace or 3-color black, ivory, and pumpkin scarf

Black and Camel
(neutral)

Black suit (pants or skirt), black shoes, Barely Black pantyhose, and black handbag with:

Camel sweater (crewneck or turtle-neck)

Camel pants or skirt (instead of black pants or skirt)

Camel shoes and Barely There pantyhose (instead of black shoes and Barely Black pantyhose)

Camel or black handbag

Gold button earrings

Gold cuff bracelet

Black and Brick
(warm)

Black suit (pants or skirt), black shoes, Barely Black pantyhose, and black handbag with:

Brick sweater (crewneck or turtleneck)

Glen plaid pants in combination gray, brick, taupe, black, etc. (instead of black pants.)

Gold collar necklace or double string of pearls

Gold or pearl button earrings

Gold cuff bracelet

Black and Plum
(cool)

Black suit (pants or skirt), black shoes, Barely Black pantyhose, and black handbag with:

Black and plum print silk blouse, or a plum silk blouse or turtleneck sweater

Plum pants or skirt (instead of black pants or skirt)

Gold cuff bracelet

Black button or hoop earrings

Brown Outfits

Brown and Cream
(neutral)

Brown suit (pants or skirt), brown shoes, Espresso pantyhose, and brown handbag with:

Cream sweater (crewneck or turtleneck) or blouse (notched collar or jewel-neckline)

Gold button earrings with turtleneck; gold hoop earrings with crewneck sweater or blouse

Gold collar necklace

Gold cuff bracelet

(Note: Always wear *gold* jewelry with brown outfits.)

Brown and Camel
(neutral)

Brown suit (pants or skirt), brown shoes, Barely There pantyhose, and brown handbag with:

Camel sweater or blouse

Camel pants or skirt (instead of brown pants or skirt)

Camel shoes (instead of brown shoes) and Barely There pantyhose

Camel handbag (instead of brown handbag)

(Note: In all the above, tan may be substituted for camel.)

Gold hoop earrings

Gold cuff bracelet

Gold chain necklace (short, heavy)

Brown and Coral
(warm)

Brown suit (pants or skirt), brown shoes, Barely There, Gentle Brown or Espresso pantyhose, and brown handbag with:

Coral silk shawl collar blouse

Camel pants or skirt (instead of brown pants or skirt)

Camel shoes and handbag (instead of brown shoes and handbag)

Gold button earrings

Gold cuff bracelet

Coral bead necklace

Brown and Teal
(cool)

Brown suit (pants or skirt), brown shoes, Espresso pantyhose, and brown handbag with:

Brown or camel turtleneck, mock turtleneck or crewneck sweater

Teal print scarf

Gold button or hoop earrings

Gold cuff bracelet

Navy Outfits

Navy and White
(neutral)

Navy suit (pants or skirt), midnight (dark) navy shoes, Classic Navy pantyhose, and navy handbag with:

White silk blouse or white silk turtle-neck sweater

String of pearls

Gold drop earrings

Gold cuff bracelet

(Note: You may substitute a navy turtle-neck sweater for the white turtleneck, or a 3-color navy, white, and yellow scarf for the string of pearls.)

Navy and Taupe
(neutral)

Navy suit (pants or suit), midnight (dark) navy shoes, Classic Navy pantyhose, and navy hand-bag with:

Taupe camisole, blouse, or sweater

Matching taupe pants or skirt (instead of navy pants or skirt)

Taupe shoes and Town Taupe pantyhose (instead of navy shoes and Classic Navy panty-hose)

(Note: In all the above, camel may be substituted for taupe)

Long scarf in taupe, navy, cream and camel, looped or knotted at bustline

Gold button earrings

Gold cuff bracelet

Navy and Pumpkin
(warm)

Navy suit (pants or skirt), midnight (dark) navy shoes, Classic Navy pantyhose, and navy handbag with:

Pumpkin silk print blouse or pumpkin silk turtleneck sweater

(Note: If you have a good tan, yellow may be substituted for pumpkin)

Gold hoop earrings

Gold cuff bracelet

Navy and Gray
(cool)

Navy suit (pants or skirt), midnight (dark) navy shoes, Classic Navy pantyhose, and navy handbag with:

Gray sweater

Gray flannel pants (instead of navy pants)

Gray shoes and Quicksilver pantyhose (instead of navy shoes and Navy pantyhose)

Silver button earrings

Silver cuff bracelet

Silver chain necklace (heavy)

You will note that in each of the above ensembles there are actually two or more outfits: the basic black, brown, or navy outfit with various tops, plus additional outfits created by substituting different color-coordinated tops, pants, shoes, pantyhose, etc. But remember, when using a suit jacket to put together an outfit, the pants or skirt should be of the same or similar fabric as the jacket.

Some additional colors that are made for each other are black and fuchsia, navy and daffodil yellow, brown and tomato red, pale gray and burgundy, taupe and turquoise, and wheat and white.

You may now use your imagination and knowledge of color to put together as many color-coordinated outfits as you like.

Prints, Patterns, and Plaids

Although solid colors are recommended for your basic wardrobe pieces, additional pieces in pinstripe, check, glen plaid, or tweed are quite appropriate. Indeed, these are often favored for office and business. The important thing is not to mix patterns.

The safest rule is to wear one pattern at a time. If, for example, the designer of your patterned jacket has not designed a separate patterned blouse (that you like) to go with the patterned jacket, wear a solid color blouse in one of your neutral or accent colors. On the other hand, you may brighten a solid color jacket with a patterned blouse or scarf in appropriate neutral or accent colors. But never wear a patterned jacket with skirt or pants of a different pattern.

Wear patterned fabrics on the part of your body that you want to emphasize. For example, you may draw attention to your upper body with a patterned jacket and minimize your hips with solid color pants or skirt.

Avoid large plaids and patterns, particularly if you are short or overweight.

Wardrobe Lists

The following wardrobe lists are presented as general guides.

Barebones Wardrobe

The components of a basic wardrobe for a working woman are:

1 Suit

1 Jacket

2 Pairs of Pants

2 Skirts

2 Blouses

1 Tailored White Shirt

1 Silk Shirt (washable)

1 Dress

1 Sweater Set

2 Pairs of Shoes (1 pumps, 1 flat)

1 Handbag

Wardrobe Building List

The following list may serve as a general guide for selecting, filling-in, and building your wardrobe. "Color of choice" means any neutral or accent color in your particular wardrobe color group,

2 3-Piece Suits (silk, wool, or wool crepe)

1 Black, Brown, or Navy (your basic wardrobe color)

1 Red (warm or cool)

1 Black Dress with Jacket (dress may be short-sleeved or sleeveless)

2 Jackets/Blazers

1 Solid (red, camel, or gray)

1 Houndstooth Check, Glen Plaid or Tweed (color of choice)

3 Skirts

1 Black, Brown, or Navy (your basic wardrobe color)

1 Camel or Gray

1 Tweed, Check, or Herringbone (color of choice)

3 Pairs of Pants

1 Black, Brown, or Navy (your basic wardrobe color)

1 Camel, Taupe, or Gray

1 Tweed, Houndstooth Check, or Glen Plaid (color of choice)

3 Blouses

    1 White or Oyster

    1 Ivory, Taupe, or Camel

    1 Cream or Black

1 Tunic Sweater (in your basic wardrobe color)

1 Sweater Set (color of choice)

1 Turtleneck Sweater (white or your basic wardrobe color)

1 Crewneck Sweater (white or cream)

1 Coat (black trenchcoat or straight boxy camelhair)

2 Handbags (1 everyday, 1 dress)

1 Pair of Black Pumps (high heels)

1 Pair of Black Pumps (1" to 1½" heels)

1 Pair of Neutral Pumps (camel, taupe, or beige)

1 Pair of Flats (skimmer or ballet)

Scarves, Jewelry, Belts, etc.

Evening Wardrobe

1 Beaded Jacket (black or red)

1 Pair of Black Palazzo or Pajama Pants (silk or crepe)

1 Pair of Straight Pants (black)

2 Skirts (1 short, 1 floor-length, in black crepe)

1 ("Little") Black Dress (crepe, knit, or jersey)

2 Camisoles (cream, black satin)

1 Pair of Black Sandals (1½" to 2" heels)

1 Evening Bag (black beaded)

1 Evening Coat (velvet, silk or fur)

1 Wrap (burn-out silk stole)

Evening is when the lights come on, and the same goes for evening wear, including jewelry. Glitter, sparkle, sheen, shimmer — all spell evening. Evening is the time to make a clean break from the day; it should be different, exciting and special!

Your evening jacket is the centerpiece of your evening wardrobe. It may be beaded, jeweled, or sequined. An excellent choice is a black or red beaded jacket because they tend to be elegantly subdued. If you select such a jacket with simple lines and the right length (approximate length of your sleeves), it should remain in style for many years.

Mix and match your jacket with all your other evening wardrobe pieces. It will be dynamite with black silk pants and matching camisole, and add flair to your "little black dress". Or you may wear only the black dress with a black beaded belt and black chiffon or burn-out silk evening wrap. For black-tie occasions, wear a floor-length dress or skirt,

Wear black hose for evening only if you wear black shoes. If you should wear gold shoes, for example, wear Barely There pantyhose; with silver shoes, wear Quicksilver pantyhose.

Beaded Jacket with Skirt / Palazzo Pants

If you plan to go from the office to dinner or a party, wear a black suit. For dinner, change your blouse to a cream or black satin camisole. For a party, change your blouse to a gold or silver lamé camisole. Add sparkling earrings, Jet pantyhose (sheer toe and heel), and slip into black strappy high heels. (If you are surprised with an invitation or pressed for time, you may do something as simple as adding earrings with a bit of sparkle to your business outfit.)

Sparkling button, hoop, and drop earrings are made for evening. Long sparkling drops are the most dramatic and should be reserved for the most elegant occasions.

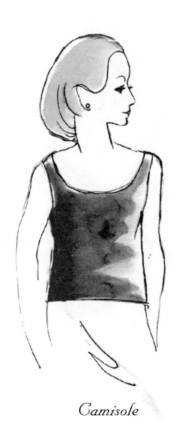

Camisole

Travel Wardrobe

1 Black Knit Pantsuit

1 Black Dress (crepe, knit, or jersey)

1 Pair of Pants (camel, taupe, or black)

1 Skirt (camel, taupe, or black)

1 Jacket (camel, taupe, or black)

1 Tunic Sweater (beige or camel)

2 Crewneck Shells (cream, beige, or black)

2 Camisoles (cream, red, or black)

2 Pairs of Black Shoes (1 dress heels, 1 flat)

1 Black Handbag (dress)

1 Extra Large Black Tote Bag

1 Evening Bag

1 Black Trenchcoat

When you plan to travel, think of a four-letter word: knit. If of good quality, knits pack well and wear comfortably. Buy the best knits your budget will allow to avoid wrinkles as well as knee and fanny springs. Synthetic wool blend gabardines also pack well and are wrinkle-resistant.

Your packing list, of course, will depend on the activities planned during your trip. To travel as light as possible, mix and match your outfits and coordinate all of them with a minimum of accessories, including one-color shoes and handbags. Take only those pieces of real jewelry you will be wearing at all times.

Pants are especially comfortable for traveling, so wear a knit pantsuit and comfortable shoes for a flight. Carry your coat and an extra large tote bag containing regular handbag items, reading materials, makeup, toiletries, and other "stuff" you might need should you arrive before your luggage.

Bon Voyage!

Wardrobe Pieces

The following is a description of various wardrobe pieces with suggestions for selecting and wearing them:

Suits

A suit may consist of two pieces (jacket and skirt) or three pieces (jacket, skirt, and pants). The most versatile is the 3-piece suit. If the cut is simple, it provides the most options for expanding your wardrobe.

If you could have only two outfits in your closet, an excellent choice would be two 3-piece silk or wool suits, one in black and the other in red or any jewel tone in your color range. When mixed with other pieces and accessories, these two suits will provide marvelous outfits for almost any occasion, day or night, such as the following:

Black jacket over bright accent color top with matching pants (red, turquoise, or emerald).

Jewel tone sweater set with black skirt or pants.

Red jacket with jeans, T-shirt and flat shoes.

Black or red jacket over contrasting color skirt/pants and favorite blouse, shirt, or sweater, with belt, scarf, and bold jewelry.

Black suit with cream or black satin camisole, sparkling earrings and black strappy heels (for evening, of course).

Two-piece Suit

Double-breasted Pantsuit

A quality black suit (or black dress with jacket) is absolutely essential for any basic wardrobe. Keep the cut simple so that the pieces will easily mix and match with your other clothes to dress-up or dress-down.

When selecting a suit, a single-breasted jacket is the best choice unless you are tall and slim, in which case you might choose a double-breasted jacket.

Dresses

Dresses are easier to put together as single outfits, but separates are more popular because of the increasing preference for pants over dresses (and skirts), and because separates can be used to put together more outfits. However, you always will need one "little black dress" in a fitted sheath or loosely-fitted chemise style.

You may buy your little black dress with or without a jacket, sleeveless or with short or full-length sleeves, and with almost any neckline. If you get it with a jacket, it will double as a suit and may be worn with or without the jacket for almost any occasion, day or night. Buy the dress in an all-season synthetic blend crepe, knit, or jersey, and always wear black pantyhose and black shoes with it — pumps by day and strappy heels for evening.

Additional dresses may include dresses of the same style as your little black dress in other colors that will coordinate with the rest of your wardrobe. Another choice is the A-line dress that falls easily over the hips and thighs and works well for those who are heavy in these areas. Straight dresses or coat dresses that hang from the shoulders, without a belt, are good for larger women, but full-body prints, patterns, and light colors should be avoided by those with weight problems.

Sheath

Chemise

Coat Dress

Before purchasing any dress, be sure the waistline of the dress aligns with your own. If it does not, do not buy it. The appropriate length depends primarily on two things: current fashion and the thinner points on your legs. Hemlines are horizontal lines that broaden the areas where they occur. Consequently, you will want your hemline to fall at one of three thinner points on your legs: just above the knee, just below the knee, or at the bottom of the calf.

Jackets

Except for suits, jackets probably will be the most expensive pieces in your wardrobe. You will build your wardrobe around them. Consequently, you should take great care in selecting the color and fabric of your jackets for versatility, wrinkle-resistant comfort, durability, and year-round wear.

You will need at least two jackets. The two most versatile colors are your basic wardrobe color (black, brown, or navy) and a warm or cool red, depending on your skin tone. When you buy your third and fourth jackets, gray flannel and camel are recommended.

The blazer (a fitted jacket) is your best choice unless you have a weight problem, in which case an unconstructed jacket will serve you better.

A double-breasted blazer is great if you are tall and slim, but if you are not, a single-breasted blazer should be your choice.

To assure a good fit, consider the waistline of the blazer first; then the shoulders and bustline. The waistline of the blazer should correspond with your own waistline. If it does not, do not buy it. If it does align with your waistline,

Blazer

Unconstructed Jacket

the length of the blazer should fall correctly near the end of your thumb. The shoulders should be sufficiently padded and squared-off to provide a smooth fit across the shoulders, down the tops of the sleeves, and from shoulder to bustline. The blazer should button easily across the bust and fit comfortably at the hip. Buying a jacket that is too tight is a common and costly mistake, so always err on the side of a loose fit.

As was previously stated, larger women should consider an unconstructed jacket; one that is not fitted. It will hang straight and have no pronounced waistline. The length is vitally important because horizontal lines broaden the areas where they occur. The bottom of your jacket is a horizontal line that is particularly exaggerated when your skirt or pants are of a contrasting color. Therefore, you will want the hem of your jacket to terminate not at the widest part of your bottom but rather at a narrower point below. Tunic-length unconstructed jackets are designed for just this purpose. Such jackets cover the problem area and their straight-hanging sides emphasize the vertical (slimming) line.

Pants

Pants are comfortable, chic, and increasingly popular for day and evening wear. They range from jeans to palazzo, but the woman at work need concern herself only with dress pants. (Jeans are appropriate neither for the office nor designed for those with large derrieres.)

Pants usually work best for those who are slim, but are quite acceptable for those who are not so slim when worn with a tunic-length jacket, sweater, vest, or other tunic top. However, pants of a soft fabric such as crushed rayon with a few soft gathers at the waistband (no elastic) will fall easily and unnoticed over fairly large hips and thighs. Add an Eisenhower jacket with shoulder pads to balance the hips, a colorful crewneck or turtleneck sweater, hoop earrings, and forget about figure problems!

Pleated pants soften the lines of a slightly protruding tummy, but they are not the solution for large hips and thighs. Nonpleated pants, when properly fitted, work best for such a figure. This may require taking in larger sized pants from the waistline to the top of the hip, reducing the waistband size, and tapering from knee to hem, leaving adequate room for the hips and thighs. If the calf is slim, keep the bottom half of the pants leg narrow to create a slim look. If the calves are full, allow enough width to avoid a tight-fitting, jodhpur look.

Whether pants are pleated or nonpleated, your blouses, shirts, and flat knit sweaters should be worn tucked in at work.

The length of your pants is vitally important. The pants legs should touch the tops of your shoes with a slight break. Too-short or too-long pants will destroy your overall look. (Too-short is probably worse.) Shoes with medium heels are best with pants.

Buy your pants in all-season synthetic blend fabrics. Never buy pants that are too long or too short in the stride. They can cause you major discomfort.

Soft-gathered Pants

Pleated Pants

Nonpleated Pants

Skirts

There are perhaps more styles of skirts than any other wardrobe piece. Relatively few styles, however, are consistently available. Among the most popular are the straight, A-line, tapered/pegged, and stitched-down pleated skirts, all of which are considered slim skirts because they are designed to produce a slimming effect.

The straight skirt is preferred by those with little or no figure problems. Still, other skirts can be the most effective pieces in your wardrobe for correcting figure problems. Although a bit of tailoring may be required, there are skirts for you whether you are too thin, too heavy, or too anything.

Dark colored A-line skirts work well for those with heavy hips, thighs, and legs. The hemline should be at the bottom of the calf, and hose and shoes should match the color of the skirt.

A tapered/pegged skirt is flattering for the slim or hourglass figure and should always be worn with the top tucked in. This skirt can also work wonders for those with heavy hips and thighs when worn with a tunic-length jacket, sweater, or vest.

Full skirts, such as gathered or circular skirts, are great for those who are super-thin or have no waistline. The use of full skirts, however, should be confined to these body types. They can look frumpy on larger body types and emphasize figure problems below the waist.

Whatever the skirt style, the hemline, as with dresses, should be located at one of the three thinner points on your leg: just above the knee, just below the knee, or at the bottom of the calf. Leave the miniskirts to the young – please!

Straight Skirt

A-line Skirt

Pegged Skirt

Stitched-down Skirt

Blouses, Sweaters, and Shirts

Blouses, sweaters, and shirts are the perfect way to add color to frame your face and expand your wardrobe after you have bought your basic pieces. For relatively little expense, you can increase dramatically the number of outfits you may put together by collecting tops in your basic wardrobe and accent colors.

Jewel-neckline

Blouses

Blouses are ideal for adding variety and color to your wardrobe. The three best styles are the jewel neckline (no collar), notched collar, and shawl collar blouses.

The jewel-neckline can be attractively accessorized with necklaces and scarves. Blouses with collars may also be worn with necklaces and scarves, as well as with vests and sweaters. All may be worn with or without a jacket or blazer, and the blouses with collars can be

Notched Collar

Shawl Collar

Crewneck

Turtleneck

Mock Turtleneck

particularly attractive when worn with just pants or skirt, belt, and bold jewelry.

The colors of your basic blouses should be ivory or white for black or navy outfits, and cream or white for brown outfits. After acquiring your basic blouses, add selections in your accent colors.

Sweaters

Sweaters include the crewneck, turtleneck, mock turtleneck, tunic, and cardigan. A twin sweater set consists of a cardigan and a shell (a short-sleeved crewneck). If made of a lightweight flat knit, all except the cardigan and tunic may be worn with a blazer or suit.

A twin sweater set is quite versatile. The cardigan and shell are designed to be worn together, but the shell may also be worn under a crisp white shirt, jacket, or blazer, and the cardigan may be worn over

Tunic Sweater

other sweaters or blouses. Tone-on-tone sweater combinations can produce marvelous effects.

The turtleneck is splendid with a blazer and pants. A turtleneck in your basic wardrobe color and another in ivory, cream, or white are great additions to your wardrobe. At least one turtleneck is a must!

Mock turtlenecks are best for those with shorter necks, but may be worn by anyone. Necklaces can be a problem, however, because they tend to override the mock turtle at the back of the neck.

Sweaters worn under a jacket or blazer should fit well, but should not be tightly fitted. The larger the bust, the looser the fit should be. Tight sweaters are out!

At work, wear your flat knit sweaters tucked in, whether your pants are pleated or nonpleated.

Shirts

The one shirt you must have in your closet is a tailored white shirt with a starchy stand-up collar. Its versatility will allow you to wear it with almost anything.

This shirt looks great with pants and pearls and is equally snappy with a gabardine suit. Tuck it in pants, skirts, or jeans, roll up the sleeves, add a cuff bracelet, and you have a winner! Or wear it under any color blazer or tweed jacket with pants, skirt, or jeans. (Needless to say, jeans are not for the office.) You also may wear the shirt as a jacket over a turtleneck, if it is of jacket length and has a squared-off hemline. A particularly striking combination is the white shirt over a white turtleneck (no necklace).

Additional shirts may be in accent colors and of washable silk or other comfortable and easy-care fabric.

Tailored White Shirt

Coats

One of the most functional full-length coats is the black gabardine trenchcoat. Other choices include the classic double-breasted camelhair or a wool blend coat with simple lines in your basic wardrobe color.

Whatever your choice, make sure the coat will fit well over your jackets and is not shorter than your skirts and dresses. To assure a proper fit, try the coat on over a jacket before you buy. Get the best fabric you can afford; you likely will wear the coat for many years.

Leather is for fun jackets and car coats.

Chapter 9

Accessories

Accessories

Accessories include handbags, shoes, pantyhose, belts, gloves, scarves, jewelry, watches, and eyewear.

Never underestimate the effect of appropriate accessories. The right accessory can transform an outfit. Just changing earrings, shoes, and handbag can create an outfit for evening.

If your leather items — handbags, shoes, belts, gloves — are of good quality, they will make any outfit look better. But if of poor quality, they can destroy the look of the smartest outfit. So always buy the best leather you can afford. There are many discount stores that can make this endeavor less expensive for you, but you must shop these stores carefully to assure quality.

Handbags

Your handbag should be in the predominant color of your clothing. If, for example, you wear camel shoes with a brown suit, your handbag should be brown. However, if only your jacket is brown and your pants, top and shoes are camel, your handbag may be either camel or brown.

You need only a few handbags. A large collection of handbags is a waste of money, closet space, and the time it takes to transfer the contents from one bag to another when you change outfits.

Choose your utility handbag in your basic wardrobe color. It will be your "everyday" bag and should be a tote or satchel large enough to carry essential items for a day working, shopping, or lunching with friends.

Your dress handbag also should be in your basic wardrobe color. It may be a small to medium-size sturdy tote, an over-the-shoulder bag, or a clutch purse. It should be simple in design, of good leather, and one you are proud to carry.

Additional handbags should be in the neutral colors of outfits you put together with your basic wardrobe pieces.

You do not need a *Louis Vuitton* to have great style and good leather in a top quality handbag. Indeed, you might find the quality handbag you want at a greatly reduced price in discount stores such as *T J Maxx* or *Ross*. But know what you are looking for and shop carefully for good leather and classic style. Do not settle for less.

All your handbags should be proportionate to your size, except your evening bag which is always small.

Evening bags come in a wide variety of styles, colors, and materials. The styles include the clutch, envelope

Handbags

Large Tote

Satchel

Small Tote

Shoulder Bag

clutch, tiny tote, and pouch. Colors include black, white, jewel tones, gold, silver, bronze, and pewter. The material may be satin, silk, brocade, velvet, mesh, beaded, or crystal. A black beaded bag in the style of your choice will be a smart selection for most occasions. Evening bags usually come with shoulder straps that may be used when more convenient than carrying the bag as a clutch.

Shoes

High-heeled pump

If you could have only two pairs of shoes, a pair of black and a pair of camel (camelhair color) pumps with 1" to 1½" heels would serve you well. They will coordinate with all the clothes in your wardrobe for almost any occasion.

In addition to your pumps, you will need a pair of flats or skimmers for casual wear (not for work). For evening shoes, select black high-heeled pumps or black strappy high-heeled sandals.

Low-heeled pump

Shoes (and pantyhose) should always be in a basic or neutral color, never an off-beat color. When your budget permits, you may add pumps in taupe, brown, tan, beige, or midnight navy. (Always buy *dark* navy shoes.) Never wear white shoes! They call attention to your feet and make them look larger.

Skimmer / Flat

When buying shoes, look for quality leather and a good fit. Stay with the brands that give you both. A quality brand that consistently fits you is a treasure.

Width is the most important consideration in getting a good fit and it can vary with your weight. Always have the salesperson measure your feet for width and length and

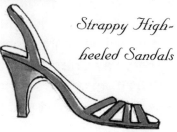

Strappy High-heeled Sandals

never buy a shoe that is not the right width. If necessary, you might settle for a half-size longer. The greatest danger is buying shoes that are too tight.

At work, always wear medium-heel pumps with suits, dresses, skirts, or pants. Pumps are preferable to slingbacks.

If, on occasion, you wear long boots, the hemline should always cover the tops of your boots. (Long boots, incidentally, can be great for those with heavy legs.)

Pantyhose

Never wear dark pantyhose unless you wear dark shoes. When possible, your hose and shoes should be in the same color.

It is a glaring error not to match hose with shoes and clothes. All of these should blend, of course, but your pantyhose color should follow the color of your shoes, not your clothes. Navy hose, for instance, are perfect with navy shoes and navy clothes. But camel shoes also may be worn appropriately with navy clothes, and in that case the hose should be Barely There, not Classic Navy.

Never wear white, off-white, or patterned hose. They call attention to your legs and usually make them look heavier, unnatural, or both.

Control-top pantyhose are recommended. They firmly hold and smooth the lines of the tummy and buttocks. However, if your work requires you to stand for long periods of time, you might consider wearing support pantyhose. They serve as a girdle and thigh-slimmer and also protect your legs if you are predisposed to varicose veins. The only problem with support pantyhose is that your color choices may be limited.

Be sure to buy your pantyhose in the correct size. A size chart is usually on each package. Ill-fitting pantyhose can cause you major discomfort.

The following is a suggested pantyhose/shoe color guide for the ever-popular *Hanes* pantyhose brand:

Pantyhose Color	*Shoe Color*
Barely Black	Black
Jet (evening wear)	Black
Classic Navy	Navy
Quicksilver	Gray/Silver
Espresso/Gentle Brown	Brown
Town Taupe	Taupe
Barely There	Camel/Tan/Brown
Little Color	Beige/Cream/Gold (and almost any other color)

Camel or taupe shoes with pantyhose in the same color will match anything in your wardrobe except black. At work, always wear Barely Black pantyhose with black shoes. Wear Jet pantyhose (sheer toe and heel) with black shoes for evening.

Belts

You really *need* only two belts: a belt with self-covered buckle in your basic wardrobe color that is narrow enough to fit the belt-loops on your pants and skirts, and a moderately wide or contoured belt in a neutral wardrobe color with a mildly decorative buckle to wear with tucked-in tops.

But remember, belts are horizontal lines that broaden the areas where they are worn. So if you have a large waistline, beware of belts that are conspicuous in design or that contrast with the colors of your outfit. If you are really large, it is perhaps best to avoid belts entirely.

When adding to your belt collection, try to find belts in the same neutral colors as your shoes. This will make mixing and matching outfits easier. However, it is always appropriate, and often desirable, to match belt color with the colors of your pants and skirts.

Gloves

Gloves, needless to say, are not the fashion accessory they once were. They now serve mainly to keep the hands warm, so buy them in your basic wardrobe color or the color of your topcoat. Select gloves of good leather or other suitable material. The less bulk, the better.

A few women still wear evening gloves, but we will let them deal with that. (Okay, evening gloves may be either long or short, in a synthetic blend fabric or leather.)

Scarves

Scarves are like salt and pepper; they enhance but should be used judiciously. You may wear a scarf with a suit, but a really handsome suit needs no such help.

The scarf's principal purpose, except for winter warmth, is to add a touch of color — not necessarily the finishing touch — to a neutral-color outfit. So collect your scarves in solids and combinations of your wardrobe and

Scarves

accent colors. You then may wear them with anything in your wardrobe.

With a jacket, top and pants in different colors, a scarf of the same three colors is striking. A short scarf tied at the neck can be quite attractive, as can a long scarf looped or knotted at the bustline over virtually any top. Solid color scarves should be worn with patterned clothes, and patterned scarves with solid color clothes. Paisley patterns are classic and particularly attractive.

You do not want your scarf to look like an add-on. The danger of this seems to increase with the size of the scarf. Perhaps the best size, except for the long scarf, is a 20" to 30" square that can be knotted at the side of your neck, or tied in back to fit inside the "v" of your blouse or suit.

Jewelry

Whatever pieces of real and costume jewelry you already have, your jewelry collection should include a selection from the following:

Pearls (16" to 18" short single; 30" to 36" long single; 18" & 20" double; 16", 18" and 20" triple strand.)

Plain cuff bracelet (gold or silver)

Plain collar, cobra, or other short (l6" to 18") bold necklace (gold or silver)

Gold or silver earrings (wide hoops, buttons or drops)

Jewelry

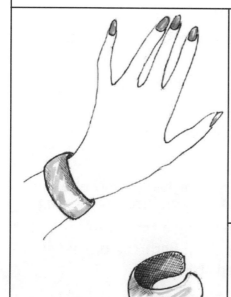

Wide Hoop Earring

Cuff Bracelet

Crystal Drop Earring

Collar Necklace

Button Earring

Pearl earrings (buttons or drops)

Semi-precious or faux stone earrings (buttons, drops, or wide hoops)

Sparkling earrings (wide hoops, buttons, drops, or studs)

Gold or silver chain necklaces (16" to 18" and 24" to 36"; medium to heavy design)

Bead necklaces in your colors of choice

If you do not have a pair of wide hoop earrings, a collar, cobra, or other short (16" to 18") bold necklace, and a wide cuff bracelet, buy these three pieces in plain gold or gold-tone and mix them with the pieces you already have. You should need little else.

Clean out your jewelry box and dispose of all fad and junk jewelry. When purchasing costume jewelry, refer to the above list and select from brands such as *Anne Klein II, Givenchy, Liz Claiborne, Monet,* and *Napier. Givenchy* and *Monet* make particularly attractive wide hoop earrings. *Gallery Design* and *Swarovski* offer marvelous sparkling costume jewelry for evening.

If you wish to shop online for jewelry, try *www.jewelrymall.com* for links to a wide variety of jewelry sites.

Earrings, as previously noted, are vital for "Framing Your Face." (See Chapter 3.) Of course, the collar, cobra, or other short bold necklace also can help frame your face.

Cuff bracelets are great with everything except evening wear.

A string of pearls is ideal with crisp white shirts, little black dresses, suits, sweaters, and blouses.

Long necklaces are good for short necks, long waists, large sizes, and are slenderizing for anyone.

Good rules for wearing jewelry are to wear fewer pieces when in doubt, and be particularly careful not to wear too many rings or layered necklaces — unless you tell fortunes.

Gold or gold-tone jewelry goes well with all colors and perhaps should be chosen for most of your jewelry. Always wear gold jewelry with brown outfits. Silver jewelry, however, is especially striking with gray outfits and is quite attractive with navy or black.

Watches

A *thin* square, round, or rectangular watch of simple design with an easily readable dial is recommended. A combination gold and silver watch and watchband is a good choice to match all your jewelry, metallic buttons, and belt buckles. However, a thin gold watch with a thin gold mesh band also is a good choice for work or evening.

Eyewear

If you wear eyeglasses, your frames are definitely an accessory. They frame your eyes, the focal point of your face, and should be chosen carefully to enhance the classy image you wish to project. A good rule is to go with fashion trends in frames but avoid extremes in shape and color.

The shape of your frames generally should contrast with the shape of your face: roundish for square faces, squarish for round faces, and oval/rectangular for long faces. But if you want to be safer, get rimless frames or frames with rimless bottoms which are usually attractive on — or at least do not detract from — most faces.

For plastic frame color, stay within the range of your neutral wardrobe colors. For metal frames, it is generally best to go with your hair color: gold frames for blonde, red and brown hair; silver frames for gray and black hair. But this is not a hard and fast rule. If you wear mostly gold jewelry, get your metal frames in gold.

The color intensity of your frames, whether metal or plastic, also should correspond generally with that of your hair. Light hair calls for light color frames; dark hair for slightly dark frames. Frames should never be darker than your hair.

The frames should be as wide as your face so that the temple pieces touch only at your ears. You also should make sure the temple pieces are long enough to fit comfortably over the tops of your ears.

The size of your frames should be proportionate to the size of your face and consistent with current fashion trends. But if you wear bifocals, remember that they may require larger lenses which, with larger frames, can make the eyeglasses heavier. So try to find a happy medium between fashion, frame size, and weight.

Chapter 10

Shopping

Shopping

Shop for clothes and accessories that flatter you! Do not settle for the ordinary or merely acceptable. Keep looking! And never buy on impulse. Before you enter a store, have a shopping list and know the maximum amount you can afford to spend.

Never buy anything simply because it is on sale or because it fits you perfectly. Everything you buy should be bought to *coordinate* with the rest of your wardrobe. Otherwise, you are wasting your money and closet space.

Mixing and matching will provide you with more outfits from fewer pieces. Consequently, you should buy fewer but better pieces. If you watch for sales, you perhaps can avoid paying full retail price for some of your pieces, but the original price is usually a good indicator of quality.

Depending on your budget, you may pay full price for everything, or you can patiently shop for bargains. The key to finding bargains is shopping at discount stores that carry at least some designer clothes and accessories, and shopping seasonal sales at department stores and boutiques.

Some sort of sale is in progress nearly all the time at most boutiques and department stores, but the real bargain sales usually occur only four times a year when the seasons change from Winter (January sales), Spring (March/April sales), Summer (August/September sales), and Fall (October/November sales). However, you must begin looking long before the sales start.

You should first visit department store designer salons and boutiques and learn to identify good quality in fabric and workmanship. Do not be bashful! Examine, study and try on suits and separates in such lines as *Evan-Picone, Jones New York, Prophecy, J H Collectables, Ann Taylor, Eileen Fisher, Ralph Lauren. Anne Klein II, Dana Buckman, Ellen Tracy,* and *St. John.* These somewhat pricey labels will demonstrate fashion and good quality in fabric and workmanship.

After satisfying yourself that you recognize good quality and fit, pick out the specific clothes you need in these or perhaps less expensive but good quality lines such as *Joan Leslie, Liz Claiborne,* or *Carol Little.* Then, when a seasonal sale begins, return regularly and track the sale prices of the clothes and accessories you selected. Their prices will be reduced until someone else buys them or until you can get them at the price you are willing to pay.

When you begin to see next season's clothes on display, it is already late in the game, but that is when you might find the best bargains. Your choices will be more limited, but if you are lucky, you may get several of your pieces for half-price or even less. Whatever the mark-down, however, never buy anything that will not coordinate with the rest of your wardrobe. Such a purchase is a waste of money.

There will be times when you find an expensive garment not on sale that you feel you cannot live without. If it fits into your wardrobe plan, buy it anyway if it will not break your budget, particularly if it is a great suit or jacket. Your wardrobe should be built around such pieces. They can set the tone and give new life to your wardrobe, while upgrading your less expensive skirts, pants, and tops.

In the meantime, shop discount stores such as *T J Maxx, Ross, Stein Mart, and Loehmann's.* You will have to patiently go through the racks to find quality labels in your size, but the rewards can be well worth the effort. If you prefer catalog shopping, try *Talbot's* or *Chadwick's of Boston* (which carries *the J.G.Hook, Willie Wear,* and *Harvé Bernard* lines).

To assure a good fit wherever you shop (except through catalogs) try everything on before you leave the store. Always check the waistline first. If the waistline of a garment does not align with your own waistline, do not buy it. Lengths may be easily altered, but not waistlines. Always err on the side of a loose fit rather than a tight fit. You will not regret it. And when you find a label or brand whose products consistently fit you, stick with them.

Buy the best quality all-season synthetic blend fabrics you can afford. They will give you year-round comfort, less wrinkles, and fewer dry cleaning bills. Linings are recommended for wardrobe pieces made of soft fabrics such as crepe, knit, and jersey. They will fit, wear, and keep their shapes better than unlined pieces.

Chapter 11

Becoming a Woman of Style

Becoming
a Woman
of Style

If you have read this book from cover to cover and understand its contents, you have the fundamentals for becoming a woman of style. And there is no better time to begin developing that style than *right now—today!*

Start the process by going to a department store cosmetics counter and asking for an appointment to get a free makeover and skin tone analysis. Then, when you return for the makeover, have this book in your handbag. After the makeover you will know your skin tone and whether you should wear warm or cool colors. (See Chapter 4.) Proceed directly to the designer salon of the department store and carefully look through the top clothing lines. (See Chapter 10.) This will help educate you on good quality in fabric and workmanship. Return at your leisure to try on clothes in these top lines and determine which colors and styles are best for you. (See Chapters 7 and 8.)

After you have made that determination, look for the right tops, shoes, pantyhose and other accessories. (See Chapter 9.)

In the meantime, search for the best hairstylist and hairstyle to properly frame your face. (See Chapter 3.) Also practice regularly the improvement of your posture and carriage to reflect a pleasant attitude of self-confidence. (See Chapter 2.)

And now, my dear, you are ready to become a woman of style. *Let your little light shine!*

Don'ts

Don'ts

The following is a miscellaneous collection of "Don'ts". You already have read some of these in the previous pages and many are obvious, but most bear repeating. So listen up!

DON'T underestimate how classy you can be!

DON'T close your mind to information and instruction that will help you develop style!

DON'T be afraid to stand out — but not too far out!

DON'T keep anything in your wardrobe that you have not worn for the past two seasons!

DON'T buy on impulse! (Know precisely what you need and how much you have to spend.)

Don'ts

DON'T wear extreme anything!

DON'T wear clunky shoes!

DON'T wear pants that are too short or too long!

DON'T wear white shoes!

DON'T wear white hose!

DON'T wear patterned hose!

DON'T wear novelty or gag clothes!

DON'T wear bold prints and patterns if you are large!

DON'T wear bold prints or patterns in full-bodied garments, whatever your size!

DON'T wear dingy-looking white clothes or undergarments! (Whiten them beautifully with *Rit Color Remover.*)

DON'T wear noisy jewelry.

DON'T wear rings on your index or middle fingers! (Too many rings say, "Don't take me seriously.")

DON'T wear frayed watchbands!

DON'T wait to buy pantyhose until you are down to your last pair! (Keep a stock of your basic colors in reserve.)

DON'T forget to smile!

DON'T forget to say "please" and "thank you"!

DON'T forget to promptly send thank-you notes for gifts and kindnesses!

DON'T forget to let your escort walk on the side nearest the traffic!

Don'ts

DON'T forget, when dining out with your escort, to be seated facing the entrance to the restaurant. (Select your choices from the menu and let your escort order for you.)

DON'T forget, when a man stands in your honor, to invite him to "please sit" when you remain standing.

DON'T chew gum in public, and *never* chew *anything* with your mouth open!

DON'T wear novel or extreme eyewear designs!

DON'T wear big hair, blue hair, or a ponytail!

DON'T talk loudly!

DON'T dress for jogging unless you are going jogging!

DON'T go out (as grandmother said) unless you are dressed as if you might meet your best beau!

Subject Index

A

ACCESSORIES
Belts 101
Defined 95
Earrings *see EARRINGS*
Eyewear 107, 123
Gloves 102
Handbags *see HANDBAGS*
Importance of 95
Jewelry
  Basic collection of 104
  Don'ts 122
  Earrings *see EARRINGS*
  Illustrations of 105
Pantyhose *see PANTYHOSE*
Quality of 95
Scarves
  Generally 102
  Illustrations of 103
Shoes *see SHOES*
Watches 107

ATTITUDE 11, 122, 123

B

BODY SIZES AND SHAPES
Balancing 43
Figure flaws, compensating
 for
  Colors, use of 46

Control-top pantyhose,
 use of 44, 100
Generally 43, 45
Shoulder pads, use of 44
Undergarments, use of
 47
Weight problems 47
Framing the body
 Front and back 44
 Side to side 44

C

CLOTHING *see also* **UNDER-
GARMENTS; WARDROBE**
Principles for selecting
 Minimize or maximize body
  area, to 46
 Slim body, to 46
Shoulder pads
 Illustration 45
 Use of 44

COLORS
Blouses, of 88
Cool 26, 54, 56
Coordinating clothing with
 skin 54, 55
Closest to face 19
Figure flaws, use of to com-
 pensate for 46, 54
Handbag, of 96

Jewel tones 57, 72, 98
Make-up, of 25
Neutral 54, 55, 57
Pantyhose 101
Scarves 102, 104
Shoes 99, 101
Skin tones, of 26, 54, 55
Tone on tone 46, 89
Warm 26, 54, 56
Wardrobe, of *see* **WARDROBE**

E

EARRINGS *see also* **ACCESSO-RIES**
Basic collection of 106
Evening, for 18, 70
Illustrations of 18, 105
Proportionate to body 18
Glittering or sparkling 18, 105, 106
Shape of 18
Size of 18

EVENING WEAR
Earrings 18, 70
Gloves 102
Handbags 96-98
Pantyhose 101
Shoes 99
Transition from office wear to 70
Wardrobe
Generally 67
Illustrations 69–70

F

FACE
Framing your 15-19
Color closest to face 19
Directing attention to 15
Earrings *see* **EARRINGS**
Hairstyle *see* **HAIR STYLES**
Importance of 15
Makeup *see* **MAKEUP**
Skin care
Cleansing skin 24
Importance of 23
Moisturizer 23, 25
Sun
Exposure to 23
Sunscreens 24
Wrinkle creams 24

FASHION DON'TS 121

FRAGRANCES 35

H

HAIRSTYLES
Choice of to balance face 16
Don'ts 123
Haircut, importance of good 17
Hairstyist, selecting 17
Illustrations of 15–16

Importance of 16
Length of 16
Shampooing hair 17

HANDBAGS
Evening, for 96, 98
Generally 96
Illustrations of 97–98
Matching to clothing 96
Size of 96

ILLUSTRATIONS
Beaded jacket with skirt/
  palazzo pants 69
Blazer 80
Blouses 87
Camisole 70
Dresses 76–78
Earrings 18, 105
Evening wear 69-70
Face 15
Hairstyles 16
Handbags 97, 98
Jewelry 105
Nails 39
Pants 84
Scarves 103
Shirt 90
Shoes 99
Shoulder pads 45
Skirts 86
Suits 73–74
Sweaters 88–89
Unconstructed jacket 81

J

JOB INTERVIEW, DRESSING FOR 57

M

MAKEUP AND COSMETICS
Application of
  Blusher 31
  Eyeliner 31
  Eyeshadow 31
  Foundation 29
  Generally 28
  Lips, to 29
Blusher 31
Caucasian women 26
Colors, choosing 25
Concealer 29
Consultation 25
Dressing table equipment 29
Eyebrows, for 30
Eyelashes, for 31
Eyeliner 31
Eyeshadow 31
Foundation 29
Lips, for 29
Powder 29
Purchasing 28
Skin tones 26
Women of color 26

N

NAIL CARE
Acrylic nails 39
Generally 39
Manicures 39
Moisturizer for hands 39
Nail polish 39
Pedicure 40

P

PANTYHOSE
Colors 101
Control-top 100
Evening, for 101
Generally 100
Keeping in reserve 122
Matching with shoes and
 clothes 100
Patterned 100, 122
Support 100

POSTURE 11

S

SHOES
Boots 100
Colors 99
Clunky 122
Dont's 122
Evening wear 99
Fitting 99
Generally 99

Illustrations of 99
White 99, 122
Work, for 100

SHOPPING
Budget, staying within 111
Catalog, by 113
Discount stores 113
Impulse buying 111, 112
Make-up, for 28
Quality of purchases 111
 Buying best you can
  afford 113
 Learning to recognize
  112
Prices 111
Sales 112

STYLE
Advantages to personal 3
Becoming a woman of
 117, 118
Defined 3
Developing, generally 4
Frames of, generally 7

U

UNDERGARMENTS
Generally 12
Using to shape body 44

V

VOICE 12

Index

W

WARDROBE
Accessories *see* **ACCESSO-RIES**
Building 51, 66
Colors
 Basic groups
  Black 53, 57
  Brown 53, 59
  Navy 52, 61
 Basic pieces 54
 Caucasian women 54
 Cool 54, 56
 Coordinating
  Examples 57-63
  Importance of 53
 Ensembles, examples of 57-63
 Jewel tones 57
 Neutral 54, 57
 Warm 54–56
 Women of color 55
Fitting of
 Dresses 79
 Jackets 79, 82
 Pants 82, 83
 Skirts 85
 Sweaters 88, 89
Good, defined 51
Importance of in workplace 52
Inventory of existing 52
List of pieces in
 Barebones 65
 Building 66, 67
 Evening 67
 Travel 71

Mixing and matching pieces in 51, 57-65
Patterned fabrics, use of 64, 122
Pieces of
 Blouses
  Basic colors of 88
  Collars of, illustrations 87
  Generally 87
 Coats 91
 Dresses
  Fitting 79
  Generally 75
  "Little black" 75
  Illustrations of 75–78
 Jackets
  Blazer 79–81
  Fitting 79
  Generally 79
  Illustrations of 80–81
  Unconstructed 79, 82
 Pants
  Fitting 82, 83
  Generally 82
  Illustrations of 84
  Types of 82
 Shirts
  Generally 90
  Illustration of 90
 Skirts
  Fitting 85
  Generally 85
  Illustrations of 86
  Types of 85
 Suits
  Generally 72
  Illustrations of 73–74

Sweaters
    Fitting 90
    Generally 88
    Illustrations of 88–89
Plaids, use of 64
Prints, use of 64, 122
Tops, use of 87
Transition from office to
 evening wear 70

WORKING WOMEN
Coordinated ensembles for 57
Earrings for 18, 104-106
Pantyhose for 101
Shoes for 100
Wardrobe, importance of 51,
 52

Notes

ORDERS

Copies of *A Guide to Style* may be purchased online at:

www.aguidetostyle.com

To order by mail, please use the following form:

Loganfield, Inc.
P.O.Box 3984
Tallahassee, FL 32315-3984

Send_____copies of *A GUIDE TO STYLE* at $25.00 $_____

Plus $4.25 shipping and handling for first book: $ 4.25
Add $1.00 for each additional book: $_____

Florida residents add 7% sales tax: $_____

Enclosed is my check or money order for: $_____
(Make payable to Loganfield, Inc.)

NAME_____

ADDRESS_____

CITY_____ STATE_____ ZIP_____

TELEPHONE (_____) _____